The Obvious Poems and *The Worthless Poems*
is a title that smacks you upside the head. So it's worthwhile to
state the obvious: James Berger may have divided his latest
book into two sections—the first of politically and socially aware
poems, intensely alive to the accelerating disintegration of
social, ecological, and ethical order in the world around us, often
descending into incandescent (and wholly understandable)
rage, the second of wordplay, formal experimentation, and
wonderfully acute, often tender quotidien observation; but his
obviousnesses are far too profound to be merely obvious, and
what he calls "worthless" is worthless only by the standards
of hedge fund managers and petrochemical investors. Once
upon a time, Horace said something about poetry being for
"instruction and delight": Berger's still working that vein,
loading every rift with ore.

Mark Scroggins

What is there to say *that we don't already know?*
James Berger, poet of the *obvious* asks; *obvious* from the root meaning
in the road, in our way, a fallen tree, or a fallen, chaotic world.

What matters now, if not simply to be here? like this enraged, compassionate,
acerbic, romantic, worried, truly human being—a scribe with a deft ear.
I dreamt I was improvising
and I was naked
not as in most dreams
(suddenly astonished embarrassed) but open, necessary, part of the music.

But I meant to say also of this poet of worthless poems, of events as
brief and insignificant as the red of a cardinal, or one's own life, or death,
I meant to say also, humble, stalwart, hopeful as well as doubtful (if not
in equal measure), happy and regnant/in movement.

Everyone has felt it, electricity of the fingers,
the merger of eyes into face-- not death,
just the shedding of context: the inhalation exhaled
as "lyric."

Billie Chernicoff

These satiric, polemical and talk-filled poems mark a chilling yet humane recognition of this obstacle-laden world, so painfully slow to enact crucial social and ecological changes. Berger's brisk work takes soundings in the systems visibly failing all around us, and he puts his findings in message-poems and bulletins to frame the necessity for transforming all this —but how? is the stark question.

Rachel Blau DuPlessis

The Obvious Poems

and

The Worthless Poems

James Berger

SPUYTEN DUYVIL
New York   Paris

© 2023 James Berger
ISBN 978-1-956005-98-1
Cover art: t thilleman, thillemantt.com

Library of Congress Cataloging-in-Publication Data

Names: Berger, James, 1954- author.
Title: The obvious poems and the worthless poems / James Berger.
Description: New York : Spuyten Duyvil, [2022]
Identifiers: LCCN 2022050970 | ISBN 9781956005981 (paperback)
Subjects: LCGFT: Poetry.
Classification: LCC PS3602.E75385 O28 2022 | DDC 811/.6--dc23/eng/20221122
LC record available at https://lccn.loc.gov/2022050970

THE OBVIOUS POEMS

"The Obvious Poems—Why?"

The Thing is Falling

Time is Money

Disintegrating Ode to a Senator

After One Sedition, Before the Next

The Work of Art in the Age of Political Breakdown

Contempt and Hatred

Addressing the Law

"This Man's Art and That Man's Scope": A Political Digression

"and admit that the waters around you have grown..."

Adapt to Dystopia

THE WORTHLESS POEMS

"Worthless poems–Why?"

What it is, what it's like, what it's not

I just saw a cardinal

It's Time, I Know it's Time

I don't own it

What's Dead on the Page

will be code [this]

I Didn't Die, Not in This World

The thing is an obstacle

a different kind of thinking

The Thing Remains

the wind is small

For Them

With Ratio/In Movement//Subjective Correlative

In a Nutshell

When a Beame was Luce New York Blacks Out, 1977

Divertimento #3

Read and Unread

Everyone has felt it

It has to be irregular

The Obvious Poems

—For Kent Johnson, above all.

"The Obvious Poems"– Why? Because they're *obvious*. What is there to say that we don't already know? The utterly dysfunctional aporetic impasse-ive sunk-in-the-abyss and anti-democratic character of our political process...is this a mystery? As Horatio to Hamlet says, "There needs no ghost, my lord, come from the grave/ To tell us this." One needs only to state the obvious. We need to eliminate the filibuster... Yuh think? So, tell Joe Manchin. Maybe he'll listen to *you*. We need to actually act to save the world as a place suitable for habitation–as in *now*, radically, effectively; create an economy not based on growth that is justly distributive. Which is obvious. But apparently impossible. But not less obvious.

This was back in the fall of 2021, when there still seemed a chance that the big Biden climate and infrastructure bill might be still at least a remote possibility–if only the screws could be put to Manchin and Kyrsten Sinema. Could it, might it happen? Was there still a real chance that democracy might be salvaged? It seemed then still in the balance. And then it wasn't. (What's that phrase? "...that government of the people, for the people, by the people might not perish from the earth"!). Perish from the earth. Yes, that's what we're talking about.

(And now there's that war... Which war? Has China invaded Taiwan, or is it still just Russia in Ukraine. Has the United States invaded anyone since publication of this document?)

And meanwhile, on FaceBook, the question was raised, what can the poets do? What ought or must they do? Kent Johnson raised the question. Why aren't we in the streets? Why aren't we writing to affect the polity? Why are we, or are we not, producing poems? And what should the poems say or do?

I thought of Shelley and his advocacy of poetry in the broad sense of all creative work that opposes the current wisdom of wealth, commodity, predation, extraction, and instrumental reason (and yes, I'm mixing Shelley with the Frankfurt School here, but they're in the same lineage). Poets are the "unacknowledged legislators of the world," and so I invented the powerful and nonexistent fellowship of the Unacknowledged Legislators: Poets for the Planet—Percy Shelley, President; myself as Recording Secretary; Kent Johnson as Social Director; Muriel Ruykeyser as Campaign Director. We actually got 237 signatures on a petition to introduce Blake's "Proverbs of Hell" as a Constitutional Amendment. I began to compose the poems that would form the prelude for our legislation. That was the beginning of the Obvious Poems.

Then things got worse.

The Thing is Falling

The thing

       is falling

          apart

The thing

       is on fire

              drowning

          shaking in weird

       spasms

The places
       where it is not
              burning or drowning

The places where
       people can live
           and grow food

[are now in narrow restricted zones passports are required
          and proofs of vaccination]

This is obvious on maps.

                         people

             cannot live

       where they are

                                    The thing

is

           falling

                              apart

the thing we live on
alive as we are alive
after whose destruction
we cannot live.

drowning

burning

This is obvious.

Time is burning. We are burning time.

Time is Money

We are drowning time

We are burning time

Time has no value for us

as if there were a Time Market,

a market for Time Futures

and there was just so much

such vast supply

that a mere hour, a mere year,

a mere century

simply had no market value,

there was so much of it–

so much Time

and whatever healing or repair, whatever change

of direction might need to be made

eventually,

could surely be made

for there is so much Time to come, Time in reserve,

Surplus Time, Time to burn.

DISINTEGRATING ODE TO A SENATOR

Can it be
that the coherent rational view
that served fairly well for such a long time

the useful forms
and ratios that bound the seasons,
continents and oceans in patterns

holding constant
across centuries, in fact, millennia,
and allowed, at least roughly, for planning–

the planting
and harvesting of crops,
building cities near rivers

and the mouths
of rivers, quarrying stone,
building ships, conducting trade

establishing
dynasties and other forms
of governance, even the beginnings

of democracy,
that most confident mode,
arrogant really, thinking that people

themselves, as they are,
possess the judgment to rule
a state together, in justice and prosperity,

across time-- (What
regularities and continuities
are required for that presumption!)--

Can it be
that these forms, modes, continuities of weather and geography,
levels of the ocean, flow of the rivers, chemistry of the air and water,
realities of soil and wind, the overall and encompassing predictability
of the world, the predictability of the world the adherence of the world
to models to models we humans can create and place on graphs express
through algorithms to every thing there is a season to every season there is
a set of characters you will chase through the grove with me we will be
pastoral past orality and will the form

                                        Drop

from under us and will some terrains and their atmospheres

find their

expression in fire in fire and other terrains and their

find their truth in deluge and inundation
                                    forking the spirit of ellipse
        to in quest
                to   then to   to

and some will

        under the forming of bridge under the

gravity sudden drop

      and no lasting form of

  impervious

    There will be war soon, is that not also too obvious.

      There is not enough planet

and it

It has no

     It has no shape.

After One Sedition; Before the Next

I dreamt I was improvising
and I was naked
not as in most dreams
(suddenly astonished embarrassed)
but open, necessary, part of the music.
I knew what key I was in, it was G
and I focused on the F#, the half tone
off the core, always back to not
quite there, in love with
the tone next to the tone–
"dissonance" yet not at all,
so close but never touching,
overtones and subtones rushing
through and past each other
an orchestra in two notes
and only one of them being played
I was only playing one note,
one naked note.

Now awake. In sunlight. In clothing.
Branches moving with changing leaves.
Faint sound of wind and friction of what touches.
Irregular squawks from birds and a dog barks.
It's a stillness, but uneven. It tilts toward
where it seems to have left.
My mind slides back toward its missing tone.
I think, it's pretty remarkable
this tendency toward harmony
from whatever assortment presents itself.

Then I think, but this isn't true.
Are you not paying attention?
What do you think is happening?
Who are these people?
Do you think they're playing?
It seems like chaos,
but really it's a knife
in your eye advertising clarity.
Do you see it now?

The Work of Art in the Age of Political Breakdown

Look any direction,
place consciousness in conjunction with desire,
play your instrument, your discipline will support you;
pull up surprise and absence--
the force of the dream–
and formal harmony
will allay
          will seem to allay
domination and ruin.

And I think, yes, the lid is off now.

CONTEMPT AND HATRED

Colossal contempt
is the abbreviation
for more complicated worries.
How much I hate them!
It's hard to put in words–
what it feels like
to see these people free and at large
unvaccinated with their guns
denying the disintegration of the ecosystems
plotting to destroy democracy,
standing on their principles of "austerity"
so the poor eat dust,
the State is suffocated
and "energy" companies are free to extract and expel
and nothing can be done nothing can be done nothing nothing
can be done to move us out of this abyss
and toward a society that is just and sustainable;
and hating education hating intellect
with no sense of empathy or even curiosity
toward the lives of others,
unaffected by the heroic beautiful struggles
of Black people for recognition, no,
hating them even more for any success,
wishing always to curtail women's lives
or the lives of any people with gender or sexual
unorthodoxies, and their ignorance, god oh god
their ignorance, how can such ignorance exist,
how can a world continue on its axis with such profound
unashamed stupidity weighing on its rotation?
Where do they think they came from

how do they think they got here
what makes them think they are the Real Americans
their piece of dirt
the "Heartland"–What *Heartland*?
Their complacency their hypocrisy their deep abounding
ignorance their lack of basic human feeling their lack
of historical knowledge their lack of basic human sympathy
for other lives what the fucking fuck.
What the fucked up fucking fucking fuck.
Fuck it. Just really.
Oh, and their preference for fetuses over the lives of people
actually walking the earth, people possessing complex thoughts
and desires and necessities and relationships,
often in conflict and contradiction, often in error
people often in selfishness often in cruelty, but also often getting
right to the mark often getting things right even
in roundabout ways and not efficiently often
with remarkable surprising kindness even capable
at times of broad solidarities, yes, of conceiving
that none of us are free until all of us are free and therefore
we live at all times in a state of unfreedom–
what a Jew would call *mitzraim*, the "narrow place"--
the place where the mind and sympathies narrow,
where the imagination is not equal
to the moral urgency required.
That's where we are.
"We"? Did I say "*we*"?
After all this preface of hatred, my unpacked contempt,
do I reach out?
What would I reach out with?
My hand? Do I reach out my hand to them?
Do I show them my face?

Do I say, I'm carrying no weapon, I just want to talk with you?
I want to understand you. I want you to understand me.
I know that at the deepest level we share one heart.
How can I not believe that?
I believe in evolution
and know that we all are one species
the differences between individuals are relatively minor
and I am, at my core, actually rather religious
and am convinced that all of us share basic
spiritual congruities, that we share, essentially,
one soul manifested in infinite bodies
the same flame burning in different ranges.
So, how can there be hatred or contempt
if we understand who we are essentially?
Well. I guess there's a long way from "essentially"
to where we actually find ourselves here in the world,
in this country, these cities and counties, this historical moment
of such immense confusion.
Hatred may be "epiphenomenal," but it sure feels real.
OK, so we hate each other and despise each other.
But, it's not our Better Angels who must have a conversation.
It's just us, somehow, at some location–
I'll meet you anywhere.
That was OBU's great idea, remember them?!
The series of small conclaves, the cultural exchange programs
between Red and Blue regions.
We've got to have this out. Very slow. Small and slow.
Piece by piece.

Small.
Slow.
Soon.

Let's talk, I mean it.

Not enough.
Bigger faster sooner.

Joe Manchin, Kyrsten Sinema, Fox News, Mitch McConnell, Jim Jordan and the whole rabble of you fucking traitorous pricks.

Addressing the Law

From now on I was thinking and the time has come
the time is now if time were something
to be spoken of in any polite or sociable way

and what I would do would be
to focus on *form*, the form of poetry.
I would do this because already

I had tried to imagine some, some what?
Some "interface"? What a lousy word–
some place of real actual legitimate genuine authentic
yes, connection, yes, I think so,

some connection that would involve my
language and my–ok, my self, ok–and...
What shall we call it? The "social
and political world"; I tried

pretty hard, though with uncertain and
somewhat incorrigible results
to write poems in something of the form
of missiles that would fly, as in a naval

battle (awkward stanza break there–
or was it brilliant? I have no idea...)
Flying into the side of the battle ship
of oligarchy and fascism
and conceptually damaging it,

blowing a fucking whole in its side.
Right. And all its prisoners would escape
like in *Fidelio* or *Cool Hand Luke*
and the damn thing would go down
it would just go down

conceptually, at any rate, conceptually
it would go down and the poems would
inspire others to take more practical turns
and bring it down for real;
transform this world; elucidate

and bring to light, shine the light on
the forms of mind the images of justice and
types of love that would open the door
to the solidarities we need, that we need

yes, that we need, do you understand–
that we need because we do not have;
the solidarities that we need to bring about
the society that we want. Simple as that.

The poem would announce, simply, clearly,
in all its obviousness and banality,
the unacknowledged legislation,

the *law*, the true obligation that we all
know but won't acknowledge and won't
act on, won't enforce as law.

And I thought, I've done that, I've done that,
I've done that as much as I could.

I want to experiment with form now.
I want to play with stanzas.

The world can go to hell.

"This Man's Art and That Man's Scope": A Political Digression

There's always someone who's allowed to be mediocre.
Maybe it's me.
I get no punishment, if no particular reward--
Only the reward of moderate prosperity,
or maybe better than moderate,
given the current state of things,
the current range of the average.
Daughters with music lessons, that's how I measure it;
that's the class division--the kids with music lessons
and the kids whose parents can't afford them.
Or sports travel-teams or chess classes
or culturally enriching vacations.
It's money beyond subsistence:
wealth, whether compact, substantial,
or beyond measurement.
That's our world now.
What can you afford?
Can you make the jump?
What will it take, how little or how much
will it take to push you under?
In those terms, I'm fine.
If our boiler breaks,
we can get a new boiler--a disturbance, not a crisis.
In fact, we'll get a really nice one, 95% efficient,
recycles heat with only that small amount of waste.
In fact, we're going to re-insulate the house--
that's a big job: good for us, good for the planet
and rather expensive (though there are incentives and rebates;
and don't get me started on the utterly non-transformative

character of "incentives" and "rebates"; our road
to hell will certainly be paved with "incentives" and "rebates")--
and our daughters will still get their music lessons.

And what's my merit?
Millions of people work hard and have nothing–
lousy heat in winter, dangerously too much heat in summer,
maybe not enough food,
and any setback threatens them with homelessness,
they can't afford fresh vegetables,
they don't know how to cook tempeh!
And their kids don't get music lessons.
Most people in this world
work harder than I do and have less.

Why is that? What have I done?

I had the right parents, yes? and then the path was clear–
to school, to college, to graduate degree,
to moderately successful career, to marriage
with a suitable, similarly educated woman,
and the two-income professional household
and two children, and a job that gives me
freedom of thought,
and both of our fathers died solvent
and left us with something not inconsiderable,
so that if we were not children of Ploutos
we also would never be poor, would never
fear poverty as a genuine possibility.
Also, I'm white, in case that was unclear.

This would be called "privilege," I think.
But might that not be a dystopian view?
That is, should not a life of moderate prosperity,
good education, mental freedom, freedom from want,
the assurance that one will not be physically attacked
by agents of the state,
and some extravagance and beauty–
children who have music lessons;
and, of course, a planet that will still be inhabitable–
should not all these be considered the *norms* of decent life,
not privileges but norms. And should not
the violations of these norms–the conditions of poverty,
servitude, violence, humiliation, oppressions of caste, poor education,
poor nutrition-health care-housing, life as struggle for subsistence--
should not all these be considered grotesque obscenities and crimes,
rather than the *default* position compared to which
a decent life appears to be a "privilege"?

So, yes, my life is one of privilege–
but only in a world whose norms are deprivation and injustice.

My privilege is that I'm required
to be no better than I am--
of no distinction, the B+ student
and middling writer, winning no prizes,
no media platform, not called upon
to comment on matters aesthetic or political,
no forthcoming obituary in the *Times*.

My privilege is to be enraged at this.

*"and admit that the waters
around you have grown..."*
–The Ancient Inundator

INUNDATE THE CAPITOL

Inundate capital.

In barges send the Obvious Poems, the Necessary Poems, the Inscrutable Poems, the poems made of lightening, the poems of water, the poems that resist all forms of breathing either by lungs or gills or whatever strange organs insects possess that bring them oxygen, the poems that will help you breathe again, the Obvious Poems the Necessary Poems the Inscrutable Poems the poems made of lightening the poems of water

INUNDATE the intersections where power assembles and disperses.

Send the poems in barges and container ships. Stuff the supply chains with poems.

TRANSMIT the Unacknowledged Legislation and the poems of anarchy the poems of chaos the poems of theory (of chaos, of anarchy... for there is no real chaos or anarchy, not in anything fabricated by human minds or hands, or perceived by them)

SEND the unending scrolling poems on the backs of joyous animal helpers–animal poets!–and SEND the poems created by Artificial Poets, some of them programed with arrogance and some with humility.

Poems will fill the streets of the great cities and centers of power and poets will wade through them, continually writing more.

Whitman will write to God to send picnic baskets, and Blake will write for shipments of ale, and Dickinson will contribute her endless notebooks in case anyone runs short of paper.

The rising of sea level will be exceeded by the rising of poetry level, and poems will absorb the sea and the coastal cities will be saved...

IF only we get there first.

The Unacknowledged Legislators achieved 226 signatures in their petition against Plutocracy.

A sad outcome, acknowledged by all the Unacknowledged. The petition went no further.

Plutocracy endured without even noticing the challenge that would have brought it down--

Now the Poets retreat to the soil and advance both downward and upward.

Now they continue to goad the Poets of Quiescence.

The Poets of Quiescence are a tremendous power. All the potential power of the Unacknowledged Legislators resides in the anxious paralysis of the Poets of Quiescence.

What will it take to goad them? Really--What will it take?!?

Are you one of them?

Where is your small mirror in the red case that says, "What am I doing today to build a Movement?"

What am I doing today to transmit the small Incantation of Sudden Adherence that will make the waves liquid and solid that will fly through the ears and all the apertures of elected rulers

and present them with the alternative that has no alternative, the alternative of

This Is What We Have To Do

and We Have To Do it Now.

ACKNOWLEDGMENT.

Thank you, Poets of Acknowledgment, Poets of Inundation.

ADAPT TO DYSTOPIA

– for Jennifer Klein

Your life is a ruin, but it's your life.

What decisions could you make better?

Do you get enough sleep, enough exercise,
      what about your diet?

Have you performed acts of kindness recently?

Research indicates that having some social contact each day,
      even if only small encounters,

Will increase your happiness.

Say hello to people. Make eye contact. Just say something
      about the weather. Give a compliment.

And of course stay in touch with your friends and family.
      Be the one to reach out.

Healthy relationships mean healthy psyche.

Be a good listener. To help others, to be kind to others,
      to be open to others

Is to be kind to yourself.

And don't keep your own negative feelings trapped inside.
　　Trust your loved ones enough to talk to them,
　　confide in them. Be open in both directions.

If you feel you need professional assistance, seek it out
　　without embarrassment. It's all right. You deserve
　　the help a professional therapist can give.

Commit yourself to your own happiness. It is not selfishness.

The more happiness you help to create in the world,
　　including your own, the better the world.

And if you think to yourself, every day the world moves closer and more quickly
　　to irrevocable ruin, each day a thousand more species are extinct, each
　　day the glaciers melt and sea levels rise, arable land is dessicated, the
　　forces destroying democracy grow stronger, the power of concentrated
　　wealth augments, billionaires have personal rocket ships, refugees from
　　zones ruined by war, tyranny, and climate explode in number, and pre-
　　dictably unpredictable zoogenic plagues shut the world down and cull
　　the human herd, and each day the forces struggling for greater equity,
　　justice, environmental sustainability move too slowly, and the chances
　　that we'll make it through this without some truly terrible outcomes
　　grow smaller...

Remember that you still are a free and autonomous person and that you still
have sovereignty over your own life, and that your happiness
is now and always in your own hands.

Your life and mind are the refuges you seek.

Reduce your stress.

Adapt.

The Worthless Poems

"Many years ago, when I began as a writer, I was fascinated with the idea of a privileged garden, a *hortus conclusus*, that would be lit only be an inner light emanating from the garden itself and no other source. I have no idea whence this vision came."

— Nathaniel Tarn, *Atlantis*

"I want to write an honest sentence. A saw cuts my thought in half, though both ends show outside the box."

— Susan Schultz, *I Want to Write an Honest Sentence*

"The letters are yeast
kneaded into an unregenerate bread.

To blaze through the frozen zone
filling zeroes with colors.
Zee and Zed. What is to be said?"

— Rachel Blau DuPlessis, *Draft LXX: Lexicon*

The world is with us—too much!

— ??

"The Worthless Poems"– Why? Because they're worthless. They begin and end, or begin and leave off somewhere that seems not to be an end, but go no further. They go no further. In one of the Obvious Poems, I determined to write no more poems that sought to engage with the world. I wrote, "The world can go to hell" and that I wanted only to write poems concerned with their own forms.

I want to experiment with form now.
I want to play with stanzas.

These are those poems. Words, elisions, juxtapositions, declensions and ascensions, annunciations and denunciations... and all spouting or sprouting from their own intrinsic and internal relationships, the play of avoidance. It can be done; one merely must set out to do it. These are the poems of the severest darkness and stupidity. Or is it the brightest lucidity? Come to my arms, my beamish boy! Not that I presume that level of exaltation.

Poetry is worthless and no one suffers for the lack of it.

I won't defend it. If I write it, it's only because I enjoy it, or really, I guess, because I believe somehow that I'm good at it and that somebody ought to recognize that fact, pathetic as it is. Fortunately, now, I realize that it's worthless.

Schiller said that Play is the zone between pure sensation and impulse–which can have no moral being–and an extreme rationality which also lacks moral sense. Play is the zone of activity in which impulse, sensation, and thought all are transformed, a zone of freedom through which the true ethical sense comes into being.

Schiller's idea of Play requires the presence or possibility of Hope. Otherwise, what would it be? It would be worthless.

I have pointed out to myself that it appears I am fishing for compliments! "Obvious?" "Worthless?" Come on, Jim, it's not that bad! I like your poems. They're neither obvious nor worthless. They're quite good. The challenges they present are pleasant ones. They give pleasure, just like Stevens said they should. Maybe they're even "interventions" into our social discourse, who knows? Or maybe they will be, some day.

And yet, here we are. This is where we are.

Ruykeyser wrote, "I lived in the first century of world wars"–that is to say, the previous century--and she wrote one of the best poems ever testifying to living in that history.

This is where we are. I'm not going to find something beautiful here.

And yet, that's alarmist, hopefully untrue... My true confession is confusion.

My friend Diane Stevenson just wrote to me,

"my body exerts
its supremacy over
rationalization, over
consolation..."

Over poetry?
As if you can just write poems at this point.
Worthless poems.

WHAT IT IS, WHAT IT'S LIKE, WHAT IT'S NOT

It isn't optimal, it isn't corpulent, it isn't vestigial
It isn't crapulous, it isn't verdant, it isn't cancerous
It isn't parodic, it isn't opulent, it isn't like a bird
It isn't optical, it isn't reciprocal, it isn't pendant
It isn't pending, it isn't fractal bending, it isn't shodden hoglike
It isn't wending, it isn't shedding, it isn't wedding
It isn't lucent, it isn't sending, it isn't optimal
It isn't reluctant, it isn't calculated, it isn't wise
It isn't wizened, it isn't frazzled, it isn't dazzled,
It isn't like a word

Is it possible that accidental leanings produce meanings
or accident loopings produce groupings or accidental blendings
mendings, do accidental liftings produce shiftings, do accidental
parkings produce markings, do accidental seemings
produce gleamings, but do accidental recalcitrances produce dances,
do accidents produce new accidents, or are they precedents?

Do accidental precedents produce testimonies?
Is every precedent an accident?
Is every act a fact, is every neglect an effect

It isn't a fact, it isn't an act, it isn't intact
it isn't cracked, it isn't checked, it isn't wrecked
Is isn't shielding we're wielding, it isn't melting you're shearing
It isn't from grimness to dimness, it isn't collage
It isn't preference, it isn't reference, it isn't deference
It isn't physics, it isn't neuroscience, it isn't genetics
It isn't history, it isn't law, it isn't culture

It isn't *Tuche*, it isn't *Ananche*, it isn't Beyonce
It isn't the Fall, it isn't the Wall, it isn't the Call

Is it possible that purposeful tics suppose bricks?
Could it be automatic, or could there be destiny in the sudden expansion?
Do wells reveal fissures reveal ores reveal cores reveal the primal weave
        reveal apostrophe reveal prosopopoeia?
Is it improvisation or is it error?
A kind of swivel?
What is the real nature of a conjunction?
Do suppressed sluices mimic voices?

        (–This poem is dedicated in secret to Michael Davidson.
        He'll know why).

I just saw a cardinal
through the window
bright bright red
scarlet crimson
on the dogwood just
blossoming pink flowers
just saw the cardinal
bright red black bill
on the thin branch
figiting bright scarlet
crimson exploded
as if a focused
blast in bird shape
red unheard of
I scrambled for my
phone in my pocket
the bird was red
and black and poking
its bill at something
and I pulled out
my phone dammit
too late

IT'S TRUE, I KNOW IT'S TRUE

How many minutes

           my egg

           another deceptive lingered

sweet potato

lurid is a word

           my egg

At the other world

           the mix, the mash, the muck
           the"m's"

Throw all the lines together

           [allow a soup]

    a code
this will be

ignites

I don't own it
I disown it.
I don't possess it
I dispossess it.
What I used to be
I've forgotten–
I mean that honestly;
but it can't be true–
I'm neurologically intact;
it's some other system
that's failing me.

What's Dead on the Page

What's dead on the page is dead on the page.
Whatever generates it dead on the page is dead on the page.
One oops two ps one-to-tive hinge probability
what is *arranged* as such is in a bloody parcel and famous
historical dead people suffer lunch around themselves
to filch and be filched of offer numerical potencies.
Always or in general mist of intangible portentous.
Don't blame the subject this is not subjective.
Imperatives derives from a prior organization internal
subject of course to standard defective outcome.
What were the previous or historical imperatives derived?
Cutting the edge poor edge.
Mirrors are mist obscurity wears paint.

Now back to weaning we're suffering milk
writing is algorithm writing is removing a hinge
Oh the looseness of the slippage between parallel
and ambient I can't choose what to repeat I
can feel at every moment a process I reject.
Introduce a topic again imperative this is my podcast.
Such feeling such decision such orbit such jettison.
Every hive gets whacked. Never be twice.

Why is this poem always telling someone what to do?
Imperative to swerve arms shot out and falling.
Why at every does? Why when a pivot signals?
Ginger is good for digestion. Chamomile for nerves.
I keep pretending that someone can do it for me.
I look at the computer and say, you know more than I do,
you have a system, if y then y, if x then not x, if noun-predicate

then adjective conjunction then decision tree optional
semantic lift up from syntax, if referent then sliding,
if door then breeze if known name then say if need
say more say more confess to mourning lie abject
in a mountain phased from common political
but tells nothing, nothing really, portent,
annunciation you can do nothing but receive
the poem opens its womb and the small named figure
dead on the page is circumvalent
I will give no name you must choose a name
choose a name

will be code [this]
space between obstacles

forecast to project [all]
wind and varies

end of one world [and]
vacancy origins

code paper [recognition]
dismantling cogs

Did you say "illusion" or "elusive"?
Nothing between nerves [asphalt]

I said the distinction was *illusive*
careful [abundance]

quick retrieval [permanent]
Which do you recognize?

Dismantle distinguish [demeanor]
brusque abundance of demeanors

The cog was permanent
its emotion was

I Didn't Die, Not in This World

I have nothing to say.
The wish flies over the mess.
Not a dialogue, there's no rejoinder.
If a picture could take the place of a thought,
      if a picture could then form in my mind
and I could tell you what it was,
and you could then say, yes, I see what you mean,
a hundred obstacles to comprehension would then
        have been hurdled.
I thought the other day I was having a stroke.
I felt odd on my left side, a weakness in my left arm,
tightness on the left side of my neck, then I thought
        it spread to my face.
I thought, no, seriously? This is happening?
I was sitting in the car in the parking lot
        of the skating rink in Milford.
My daughter was inside skating.
My wife was in California at a conference.
My other daughter was at home.
I thought, if this is happening, I need to call 911.
I Googled the symptoms of stroke, these all were symptoms.
        And why not? It was entirely possible.
And it was so weird, could it really be this?
I tried to be calm--
I thought, I'll drive to Starbucks and get a latte.
If I can do that, I'm probably ok.
So I did, and I got back with the latte.
And I went for a walk out from the parking lot
        into a little piece of woods adjacent to the rink,
drinking my coffee. I had to pee, so I found a spot

behind some trees and peed.
And I got back and still felt a little strange, but less now.
I thought, it's probably just tension; end of term, Jen
      in California,
the girls with all this stuff they're doing and they're stressed out
         with music recitals, taekwondo tournament, skating performance,
         a lot of homework, they're reading *Frankenstein,*
which is great, but difficult, and the English teacher
      gives them lots of assignments to go with the reading,
      they're up till midnight every night.

And somehow I'm feeling all of it with them, plus I'm
      driving them everywhere--
And I said I wasn't going to mention the world anymore in my poems,
      so I won't, no, but there it is—the war...
which war? What year is it? You can decide... is it our new
      Civil War? Has that begun? Do you think it's begun?
Or is it just the accelerated collapse of the biosphere and our
      fumbling grim denial of it—
But I said I wasn't going to write about the world.
I'm shutting down, and this is me, in the car
      having a stroke.
I'm not having a stroke. OK? I'm not.
But I could be, and I'm completely not ready.
There's stuff I need to delete and throw out, I need
      to have my persona resolved
      and archive my papers. I need
      to finish my work.
I can't just die in the car in the parking lot
      and Teya comes out from skating and finds me.
I didn't die.

I drove with Teya home. The day was gorgeous,
    the first really warm day of Spring.
I thought, I'll see for sure. I'll go for a bike ride,
    I'll ride fifteen miles, really air it out,
and that's what I did.

THE THING IS AN OBSTACLE

like fallen trees.

They stop a road, but not a path.

On the path, you bend down and slide under one

then jump or hoist yourself over the next

and you get by.

In a car, you can do nothing.

Turn around. Wait for the road crew.

The obstacle, as if it had a mind,

selects your adroitness; if you can't do it,

you wouldn't be on the path. If

you're there, you can do it.

Why should there not be a fallen tree on the path?

The road's premise is lack of obstacle.

The car has no adroitness.

a different kind of thinking
a different weighing
it accompanies me
as heaviness
Heave junction
cleave disjunction

hove

The fox ill trot
the miising key wweave
twd rabbit fixed in spot
Kerneling fixing
the shoulder breathe
lying down in the street

I'm learning it

THE THING REMAINS

The thing that
for just that moment
locked its sentience--

Against what?
would stagger with wind
knocked out of them–

Outside all is light, inside is light.
Swing till you're dizzy and fall,
things you jump on and whirl,

laid out, always expanding,
expanding, in journals, industries,
entireties, noise and closeness,

checkout lines, subsidies, traffic,
sound systems, wifi, nooks for conversation,
in public places in rooms with light.

But who slammed into that thing?
Can I, with the right tools, configure conduits–
Which place is more real?

I don't know if you can breathe there,
I haven't tried.
Available to some other sense

it has qualities of a vacuum.
I don't know if there is vibration.
The thing remains dark,

not illuminated, unread.
Looming presumed, slamming it properly,
invoked, inveighed--

The barrier would stop you.
                             You?
One would be stopped.
                                   One?
It would.
                                            Would it?

the wind is small
pink blossoms yes
a lot of them
in motion
a moving picture

of joy, there could
be a word
I'm missing
to say what this
is, colored motion

****

moon wind derives
not moon wind
from hence
to whither
swift lunacy

cirrhus flash
of clear rushing
blinded cargo
thrown and
there blown

FOR THEM

I'll realize
it was always for them
I thought it was for me
My ego immortal
I could stand
on both sides of the boundary
define myself
create the terms by which
I would be known
A limit could not be a limit
not really; conceptually
I could always surpass it
But that conceptual surpassing
presumes a mind
that also knows no limit
The infinity of the concept
is deranged by the finitude
of the mind conceiving
When I step to the limit,
if I see–what can I call it?
If this were sci-fi, it would be
a "portal"–...if I encounter
a *portal* and I step through it,
I will not then move past
the limit that had been
my limit
I will be somewhere else
I will not be "I"; my neural networks
will collapse with the rest
of my biology

It was always them, always for them
It will be their judgement
that I will never hear.

WITH RATIO

with ratio
surprising the gratitude
holding flanks
in the tiny theater
jumps through our courage
as their sorrow
to sing
so incommensurate
in senses of clearness
a memory tangled
in the tiny theater

SUBJECTIVE CORRELATIVE

And yet

are

has not flowered,

Roots branches flowers;

a town, adjacent
to a city, part of the city.

relations

WITH RATIO

       do you blue bowl
wooden spoon
larger than
Empty the space
to be pertinent is to be cookie batter
(It does jump, it does)
at the entrance she's smiling broadly
but several objects
no *thought*
have you forgotten your precision?
To pertain

SUBJECTIVE CORRELATIVE

        as "rejoicing"?
of the voice? Could it be felt
as"mourning"?
Why does it feel
how it is felt?
There is nothing abstract about
abstracted, can be
discrete and
nothing is ever still.
No shape you could call a "form."
Wind and light give color.
Some immaterial thread.
Nearby stands a tool shed.

WITH RATIO

Now do you

           Now do you

       Now do you

Now do you

              Now do you

         Now do you

Now do you

SUBJECTIVE CORRELATIVE

         I could have searched
For hours, for years, for a lifetime

On opening the book.
that first found my eyes
not found the words
almost clairvoyant,
Which seems
to add to the bewilderment
opening to a random page
memory
differently textured–
unraveled.
Why like this,
Why this, why this?

And each thing
that flowers
loss
of never loss
the running spectrum
Memory
the tree
of cognizance
The tree

is separate
is joined
Is separate
opens
This live thing,
it had been shut,
and then the street
the tree
Sudden cognizance
not recognized
the tree
Bent from form
the tree
disparity
Correlation

the tree
of the element
In a fraction
that flowers
has flowered

except

WITH RATIO

in hoof marks, lattices
in inventory, brushed trunks
in story, movement
wooded areas bordered by massed birds
congratulating with many arms
canister pavilions onto a stage of quick development
the animals as banisters
to be grieving, to jump
to be reviving in density
To be happy and regnant
in movement

In a Nutshell

In a forest it seems always to begin,
the nutshell of infinite space,
a matter of mechanics, really.

She doesn't want to die, she wants to live.

Did you retreat from dimension?

The bird can't fly out of your sight.

In the fabric of sublimity
you are never stuck.
My perimeter is sketched inside me.
Phantasms of *with*.

She was exploring the methodical sadness of shellfish.

When the Beame was Luce
New York Blacks Out, 1977

I perched this carp onto a flounder:
Yes, two brains, we have two brains
and our skins are black or red or
brown--the mystical relation
of the sun's bombardment.
Who you are, what you're about;
there are some people who can't sit still
or who like things neat and clean
of who just like to fight.

The dutiful sun
rises at night.
Women tie up their hair
and go to bed early.
Voice of a dog is a command.
Sex is the original--
A line breaks; long brown hair.
A horrifying implant of certain knowledge.
A ferocious masturbation, and then, daily,
to an understanding and a resolution.
If not for-- There could be no--
The dog knows-- that this pleasure-- that seeing--
is defilement.

The ground lags,
hangs in its valleys.
The huge orange projects
softly rise. Hot thick air
melts their edges.

The city is melting.
The bus passes by the projects,
manacled to their shadows,
138th Street, the huge stillness.
The streets are empty.
Harlem is empty.
At night it burns.
Deserted cars, garbage,
decays.

Every night a block burns,
the sky is full of bright ashes,
and people gather to watch the city shine
and shrink.

On the radio, the Mets are playing at Shea,
and then they're not,
and it's all dark and everything is groping
nothing is solid, but windows and metal gates.
Darkness is free,
everyone can have some. Power costs money,
but the blackout is free, and everything
inside the dark, every store is open
and every impediment and power grid
is down. Beame and Luce have a loose beam
and 3,500 had to be tightly latched
for beaming when luce
went out.

In the darkness, chaos is the facsimile of justice, since light is oppression.

Abe Beame (1906-2001) was mayor of New York City from 1974-77. Charles Luce (1917-2008) was Chairman and CEO of Consolidated Edison from 1967-82. At 9:37 PM on July 13, almost all of New York City lost electrical power. In the darkness, there was widespread looting. At Shea Stadium, the Mets were losing 2-1 to the Chicago Cubs. Between July 29, 1976 and July 31, 1977, David Berkowitz (1953-present, aka Son of Sam) murdered six people in New York, five of them women.

DIVERTIMENTO # 3

Most of my poems are bad, I can see that.

When I look back at older poems,

try to retrieve something, *something* from all that activity

or ambition or flailing around

with the idea of poetry or experience

or following the woozle-trail of each word

creating its impression but what seems

to be sequence is a melting circle

that steps on itself...

Well, it doesn't work.

There's barely a line that works.

Sometimes a line almost works, but never quite thoroughly.

They're bad.

I didn't see it. Then I saw it. Now it's clear.

And so it's a good thing, good for the world,

or the world of poetry, I mean,

that I've accomplished so little

in terms of acclaim or recognition.

So much less waste.

What if I were one of those poets whose every poem

is deemed publishable, and *is* published,

and who publishes and can publish anything

that comes off his fingers, who puts together

every year or so his latest *project* of formal or thematic

invention and has it respectfully added to the pile

of respected projects by respected poets?

Oh, look at Berger's latest thing.

Wow. Nice. He's good.

True that. He did a blurb for my friend's book.

But you know, I liked his fourth book–I think it's his fourth–

better than his fifth. That's the one where
every third word is a bird and each stanza
begins with an anagram from a speech
by that Rojavan guy in prison.
I think maybe
he's running out of ideas.
I know, but I still want to study with him.

READ AND UNREAD

(through reeds).
Red/Unred.
Some colors are signals
some design--
patterns enunce port-
end partic-
ulate general
pointings.
There is price
between inter and
predation,
accost to redeem
what means?
Can you interpret for me?
The meaning will not be
what you intend
or send
or what I receive
and configure--
Is there nothing precise here?
What's carried
over sent across thrown
forward
bounced back?
There is nothing precise here.
It's all unred, about to be red,
but for the blue note
tagging the last syllable
and the green fruit
you should not eat
yet.

Everyone has felt it,
electricity of the fingers,
the merger of eyes into face--
not death,
just the shedding of context:
the inhalation exhaled
as "lyric."

It has to be irregular.
Structure is internal,

encoded. The message
is its action, result

as division, replica
as cell sweet energy

that can gird,
frisks no matter how

empty the space
larger than--

within, so huge
from place to place

no idea or feeling
of compulsion

sudden abundance of thought
for no reason

axial thought.

JAMES BERGER'S bios continues, but feels increasingly detached from its graphein. Nonetheless, he lives in New Haven CT and professes, at Yale, Literature and how it got there. This is his third book of poems—or maybe his fifth, depending on what category the *OBU Manifestos* books are to be placed in. He has written two scholarly monographs. He works now on "The Book of Impasses," concerning our imaginative failures to conceive a just and sustainable future, which includes, at a lower pitch, his failure to write the book. He is married to a historian, Jennifer Klein, which does give him some hope for the future; and is father to two daughters, Hannah and Teya, who are now better musicians on violin and flute than he ever was on his glad euphonium; and they give him more hope.

These are his books, to this point: *After the End: Representations of Post-Apocalypse* (U. of Minnesota Press, 1999); *Prior* (BlazeVox, 2013); *The Disarticulate: Language, Disability, and the Narratives of Modernity* (NYU Press, 2014); *The OBU Manifestos* (Dispatches Editions/Spuyten Duyvil, 2017); *The OBU Manifestos, vol. 2* (Dispatches Editions/Spuyten Duyvil, 2019); *Under the Impression* (BlazeVox, 2020). He also edited and wrote the introduction to *The Story of My Life: The Restored Edition* (by Helen Keller; Modern Library/ Random House, 2003.

www.ingramcontent.com/pod-product-compliance
Lightning Source LLC
Chambersburg PA
CBHW011217120626
46545CB00008B/3030